When Nature Nurtures

When Nature
Nurtures

Written and illustrated by

Lizzy Paylan

T

Copyright © 2024 Lizzy Paylan

The moral right of the author has been asserted.

Apart from any fair dealing for the purposes of research or private study, or criticism or review, as permitted under the Copyright, Designs and Patents Act 1988, this publication may only be reproduced, stored or transmitted, in any form or by any means, with the prior permission in writing of the publishers, or in the case of reprographic reproduction in accordance with the terms of licences issued by the Copyright Licensing Agency. Enquiries concerning reproduction outside those terms should be sent to the publishers.

Troubador Publishing Ltd
Unit E2 Airfield Business Park,
Harrison Road, Market Harborough,
Leicestershire. LE16 7UL
Tel: 0116 2792299
Email: books@troubador.co.uk
Web: www.troubador.co.uk

ISBN 978 1836280 972

British Library Cataloguing in Publication Data.
A catalogue record for this book is available from the British Library.

Printed and bound in Great Britain by 4edge Limited
Typeset in 11pt Aldine401 BT by Troubador Publishing Ltd, Leicester, UK

For my Son Tom, I have finally done it!
For all your love, support and encouragement
For everyone I Love, you know who you are!

'Crawdads' Monsters of the Riverbank

Today I'm going signal crayfishing. My friend tells me about a lake that he fishes with his son, and that the river Windrush almost adjacent is full of this invasive species, they are terrified they will colonise the lake. Sometime in the 1960's they were introduced from North America supposedly to help with the crayfish plague... turns out... they are the carrier of the disease. Yet another bright intervention on man's part! And we are the ones with the brain!

This will be a totally new experience for me. I think I'm prepared; I have stinky old bacon for bait, a stick as a rod, some string for my line, my wellies and bucket in case we catch.

On the journey I ask how big can they get? "Ah! They can reach up to 15cm long, they're aggressive and ruining the banks by burrowing deep into them. They eat anything and everything, aquatic plants, fish eggs, so nothing has much chance."

"Sounds horrific."

"It's actually illegal once caught to put them back." I've never heard that before.

We park up, it's only a short walk to the river. It's August, warm, but it rained in the night, I'm glad of my wellies. As we lower ourselves down the bank, the damage is immediately obvious, no vegetation, no river weed, just mud, murky water and holes in the bank. Gosh! I'm not sure what awaits me! We tie our string to our poles, our stinky bacon to the end of about ten foot of string and drop it at the water's edge. The bacon rocks gently back and forth in a few inches of water, spreading its stinky aroma.

For ages nothing happens.

Then there is movement in the mud, the water clouds from disturbance.

Big powerful claws appear and then the rest of him, it is so well camouflaged, dark muddy brown, only a hint of white above his pincher giving him away. It moves slowly towards the bacon. "Wait till it has a tight hold," I'm advised.

As I watch other areas in the mud cloud up with disturbed silt and more creatures emerge. It is like a horror film. The first one on the scene has got the bacon and is trying to take it back to his burrow. I raise my line slowly; he is clinging to his prize. I have a bucket ready, half full of river water, suddenly aware something is not right, he releases the bacon… too late, with a splash he lands in the bucket, I jump! Panicked, he scurries around the bottom of the bucket, clawing at the plastic sides to escape. I watch him and shudder. It really is prehistoric. News travels fast, as I drop my bacon back in the river they are coming from everywhere. Climbing over each other, pushing and jostling, tearing chunks from the bacon. I lift my line, five hang on. I squeal… two drop back into the water, three land in the bucket. The first one already in, is unimpressed and raises his pinchers in protest.

I put a bigger piece of bacon on and plop it back out. Before an hour is over, I have eighteen. Enough for a meal or two!

On the journey home, the bucket is in the foot well, between my legs, they are quiet and motionless.

Once boiled, they turned bright orange, perfect little lobsters, much more appetising. Not much meat disappointingly seeing the damage they've done to the rivers; all guilt evades me.

When can we go again?

Venturer

The minibus engine hums gently, as I press the control button for the hydraulic hoist... it clangs shut. Everyone on board. Picnic packed in large bright blue heavy-duty hampers, wedged safely behind the front seats.

Two colleagues and I are taking a group of our elderly residents out for the day on a narrow boat. She is moored and waits patiently for us in a boat yard near Jericho in Oxford, on the canal we will travel up towards Iffley lock, then out on the Thames and along Port Meadow. Common land where the horses and cattle graze, on hot days they cool themselves, knee-deep where the bank slopes gradually. Flocks of geese and swans graze the cropped grass in harmony.

We have a happy selection in our box today, they have been looking forward to this for days. We take our residents for pub lunches, shopping trips and the theatre, but the river trip with picnic is the summer favourite. Today some are on sticks, some on frames, one gent who stays in his wheelchair and Joan who lives in the moment.

I have a new colleague too today, who has yet to experience the fun of a day out.

"Just watch for today, observation is far more helpful at this point," I tell her. She watched the ramp go up and down, the bus filled, excited chatter and laughter from us all.

I swing myself into the driver's seat and look at her. "What do you think so far?"

"Well, if you could film it, speed it up and play it to Benny Hill music," she replies. We laugh, we are going to get on just fine. My other colleague is a nurse. I am always relieved to have her onboard, we carry a precious cargo, over five hundred years of experience and knowledge.

The narrow boat we are travelling on is called 'The Venturer'; she is designed and equipped for the less able among us, with ramps and hydraulic hoist to lower us below deck. Two friendly, supportive volunteers steer and open and shut the locks we pass through, and provide us with canal and river information. We provide refreshments and lunch, and probably comical entertainment, down their local, once the day is done.

Everything we require is on board, it is very well thought through, cooker, fridge and endless cups, glasses, and plates, so we can have hot teas and cold wine with lunch.

The toilets are another story, when dealing with our elderly clients, we manage somehow. We couldn't have asked for better weather, but just in case we have all bought the appropriate wet weather gear. I remember one trip we unloaded the boat dressed in black bins bags, it doesn't look like we will need it today, but it does get cool out on the water.

Once we are all settled, teas and coffees drunk, happy chatter emanates, we reminisce of days of old, sailing holidays, boat trips with loved ones and children.

One of the volunteers instructs us 'firmly' that at no point should anyone's hand hang over the side of the boat, there are no brakes! We will have to be alert, not that anyone is going far without our assistance. Several of our group wish to be outside at the helm, in the sun. There is plenty of room, several chairs already placed for this purpose.

A fabulous viewpoint as we travel through the water. We can see into people's back gardens; many have canoes and small boats moored on small jetties. As we travel alongside the tow path, brightly coloured barges are moored, and we comment on their names. Some have gardens on their roofs and cats sun themselves. One boat has a sign painted along its side, 'May contain nuts'. I need that on the minibus, I tell them, we all laugh.

The tow path is well walked, people we pass wave and smile, joggers, dog walkers, lovers hand in hand. The occasional fisherman looks up as his line is jostled in our wake.

The ducks' orange feet paddle relentlessly towards us in the hope of a crust of bread. There will be plenty of leftovers after our picnic lunch. They stop paddling and glide into the reeds.

Then from out underneath the trailing willow branches a magnificent Great Crested Grebe floats elegantly alongside. It is a resident of the UK, but we've never seen one this close-up. We all watch... it's about the size of a large duck with a long white neck, black ear tufts and a chestnut neck frill, a bright yellow sharp bill with piercing orange eyes. Just beautiful. He is only a few feet from us. Suddenly he disappears under the dark water surface, seconds later he reappears with a large brown carp in his bill, the water cascades down his neck and back, dissatisfied with his catch, he flings the fat carp – 'splash', it breaks water and dives back to the dark depths below, lucky escape.

Grebe dives down beneath the surface again, reappearing several yards upstream, he has in his bill a beautiful silver jack pike. He holds his head skyward and swallows, down in one. A quick head shake, a moment to compose himself and he paddles off back towards the overhanging willows. "Did you see that?" one of our ladies asks. "He didn't like the first course."

The day was a great success, no injuries or incidents, the weather stayed fine.

Many slept after lunch, so my colleagues and I rested in the fresh air. Joan stayed awake and with us, enjoying every moment.

The hedgerows were bursting with the biggest, juiciest blackberries I have ever seen, unreachable and unspoilt. The crew as usual were helpful, fun, and kind.

Once back home, everyone comfortable back in the familiarity of their own rooms, it is a long day for them, but worth every moment. I thank the kitchen staff for a once again perfect picnic.

I return the bus to her parking place under the great oaks, ready for her next adventure. I just had to return the keys to the nursing wing, back on its hook. Joan who had enjoyed and stayed awake all day was hovering at the top of the stairs, lost. I thought of her standing at the helm on the boat, her smile as the sun kissed her face, her silver hair tussled in the breeze.

"Have you had a good day, Joan?" came a deep voice from inside the office.

"No! nothing ever happens here" she replies lowering her head sadly.

My manager meets eyes with me and smiles. "One of the perks of the job?" I offer. I hang up the keys and head for home.

Splash! And it was over

"Today I feel hopeful," I've been saying this for years, and still never caught that ever elusive salmon. It is a turquoise blue, cloudless sky, fresh and clear still a nip in the air but the potential to be boiling by midday.

We are fishing the Gwili River today, a tributary of the river Tywi in Carmarthenshire. We, my boyfriend, and I have chosen to fish a spot called 'The Ladders', we park in a quiet spot on the side of a B road, pulling the car up onto a verge. Rods already set, we drop down the bank and under a narrow underpass; there are dried cloven hoofprints and dried dung, signs the farmer uses this to drive his cattle to and from the lush green meadows, avoiding any traffic, beyond the hedge line is the river. Thankfully the walls of the underpass have not yet been visited by the graffiti artists, it remains unspoilt. The gravel track leads to a gate, that opens easily, I'm relieved and excited to get to the river, the feeling of what the river will surprise me with is as always intoxicating. My pace quickens. I'm fishing light today, I have treated myself to a fishing waistcoat, beige, light weight with many pockets. My fishing licence and permit in my breast pocket in case the bailiff appears, as they do on occasions. Some extra line, a few lures, and a priest in my front pocket. A priest is a small club, mine is about 8" long, plain wood with a solid steel head, used to dispatch the fish. When caught, one quick knock on the back of their head, sounds awful but beats flapping on the bank gasping for breath. I only take what I will eat, anything else is released back into the river.

I've chosen to spin today; the water is clear. Spinners mimic the fishes' prey. They come in many colours, forms, and disguises. I have a hexagonal glass pasta jar I found in a charity shop, it is full of lures and spinners, hooks, and weights that I have found over the years in hedgerows, overhanging trees, buried in the sand or snagged between rocks, quite a macabre collection. Once your spinner is attached, you cast out across the river and slowly wind in your line, hopefully the fish will make a grab for it. I enjoy spinning, it is tiring, you are on the move again once you have cast across the river several times.

We move on to another stretch of river. There are four rivers that I have fished over the years that I know better than any other places, where the deep pools are, where the snags hide waiting to grab your line and where the salmon lie, but this does not mean you will catch one.

Today I'm using a flying C, it's about three inches long, red, rubber coated, frayed at the tip and looks squid like.

My small fishing bag from the army surplus shop hangs over my shoulder, water and sandwiches and my smoking apparel inside.

The meadow grass is long, nearly knee-deep, untouched as yet by the cattle, they will be like kids in a sweetshop when they come through the gate finally. Experience has taught me to wear waterproof trousers, a real godsend, when sitting on damp rocks or sliding down banks. We cross the field together, both in our own thoughts. We leave a dark green path in our wake as we walk through the lush buttercups and clover, so green it could be velvet, until we reach the hedge line. The fishing clubs take great care of their waters. Car parks, signs, gates, and styles and today ladders are all well maintained. As we move through the trees and in a few yards the bank drops steeply below, the river glistens, quiet, undisturbed.

Heavy duty ladders have been secured to the bank, three of them, we choose the most accessible. I pass my rod down. I'm not a fan of heights, but I climb down, heart racing, watching every rung.

I focus on the bank itself, ferns and ivy, tiny white and blue wildflowers, tree roots protruding from time worn soil providing extra grab support. Once on solid ground I turn, it's always a magical spot, probably because it's not easy. Our boots crunch on the fine shingle shoreline, it is like a secret secluded bay. The river to the right heads off fairly straight on its way to the Tywi estuary and then onto the sea. To the left, it curves around a shingle spit out of sight, carving her way through the hills beyond. Here just down from the ladders, where I intend to fish, is perfect. It's warm only a gentle breeze tickles the water surface. With a good long cast, I can just about reach the far side, there the water is dark and faster flowing, willow bow their branches, creating cool shade. If I were a fish I'd swim there, pure bliss.

The boyfriend has disappeared off around the bend out of sight. I sit on the shingle, roll a cigarette, and watch the river. A few mayflies, long legs dangling, have made it into the sunlight and flitter above the water surface. Small trout jump in the distance, leaving behind a circular rippled pool as they disappear beneath the surface, cattle moo and tractors work far off in the valley beyond. All thoughts of work and responsibilities gone, the sun glitters on the surface of the river and my face tingles in its rays. I walk to the water's edge and cast out. I love the sound of my line spinning off the reel 'tzzz' and the plop of my spinner as she breaks through the water surface. I let it float momentarily with the current, then slowly wind her back in across the river. One can only imagine what is happening beneath. I cast several times, criss-crossing the river, pulling my lure through the water.

I move and cast downstream, letting the current bring my line across. Suddenly, not far from where my line disappears under the water surface there is movement in the river. Furry, sleek, beady eyed, heads popping up and down, close enough I can see water droplets from their whiskers. Dear God! It's an otter and not just one, she has two cubs with her, they are oblivious of me. Nuzzling and pushing and twisting around each other as they travel ever nearer.

I very slowly wind my line in and lay my rod down by my side. I have never seen wild otter before, only their tracks. They are so graceful, so enjoying their time. I can see the mother smiling with pleasure and pride. How lucky am I.

Splash!!! A horrendous splash and a whirlpool size circle is all that remains in the river surface. They vanish without a trace.

I stand there shocked, stunned, mouth open and then I sense a presence behind me, and I turn; standing there behind me is my boyfriend, chest puffed out with two more large rocks one in each hand. If my eyes were a loaded gun, he would not be with us now!

"We won't catch any salmon with them in the area," he blurts out.

For me it's over, a sudden awakening, I am so with the wrong guy. I'm still trying to register what has just happened and the selfishness of it all. I'm stunned! When I can finally speak, I simply say, "The salmon would be have long gone, even before we got here." There is no point
 to continue fishing, everything in the vicinity would have been spooked by either otter or rocks.

We climb the ladder, head back to the car. Sometimes saying nothing says it all!

Leap of Faith

Time had moved on since the otter incident.

The atmosphere had not improved and there was the realisation we didn't make each other happy. Thankfully I had a job I loved, I had slowly gathered enough money to move on. My son had grown up, had a good job, good friends, girlfriend and was rarely home. I could finally leave. The decision was easy.

"No point flogging a dead horse", the boyfriend's words. I had already spoken with my manager at work, they had offered me a room, tiny but a 'safe haven' in the grounds. Somewhere to gather myself. I hadn't yet told him I was moving out. I had one last trip I wanted in Wales. In all the years fishing there, I had often suggested being on the river at daybreak, as the light rises over the valley and turns the river to gold. In my mind, it had always been the Cothi River, the hardest river I've fished. It is bedrock, deep gullies, a young man's river. Rumour had it, occasional bodies were found, washed down from the asylum several miles upstream; thankfully I never came across one. It has fast flowing rapids, narrow ravines, precarious climbs down steep banks, slippery rocks covered in moss and weed, to quieter pools and calm waters, as the river winds her way, where the salmon rest.

I know in my heart, once I leave, I may never see these magical rivers again or not for a very long time. It's a Saturday evening, I tell him I'd like to be up before dawn, fishing by sunrise. It's a good half an hour drive, off the main road, climbing up hills, then dropping down narrow lanes, following at times the course of the river, at others crossing over it. There is a very narrow bridge, iron, one car's width.

You have to approach it head on; this involves pulling into a lay by and facing the car straight ahead. Isolated farms and houses dot the landscape. The narrow lanes lead down, foxgloves and primrose line the banks. Then you reach the farm with a field of white geese and pull into the fishing club carpark. Great oak, ash, and chestnut shade the river below. The granite shingle floor of the carpark is mossy and slippery. It is dark cool and mysterious down there. Huge tree roots, lie exposed in the earth, huge boulders, tall ferns. I often imagine 'Smeagol' from *Lord of the Rings* popping up from behind a large rock, indicating with his gross finger to follow him "My precious". A land that time forgot. In complete contrast, the sun above the tree line and the raging river below, it can feel a good 10 degrees warmer. Here sheep and cattle graze, a well-trodden path follows the rivers course. A few years past on a Christmas day, we came just to look, it was a freezing, snowing, a treacherous journey. As we crossed the river, I saw my first leaping salmon, lunging up the rapids, in a split second it vanished amongst the spray, for my eyes only.

The Reese pool is a calm spot to fish, an old tree root has formed a cosy nest, filled over time with silt from flooding and ferns and wildflowers have grown, it is just enough for one and protrudes out over a pool. I had engraved my initials in the root a few years back when I got my first Swiss army knife. The trees are sparse here, so it's warmer and a good place for lunch. The water speeds up a little farther on, narrows and races and clashes between huge, jagged rocks, if you went in, you won't be coming out. There are several styles to climb to get to the Reese pool and gullies rush down from the hillside, one crossing point is just a plank across a gully, I dread this crossing, and hang on to young sapling branches, it's a long way down. Thankfully the fishing club have made a support rail in recent times. It's a young man's river! I can't sleep thinking about it.

I am restless for the off. I get up and dress, everything is ready by the back door. "What are you doing?" a grumpy voice asks. "Getting ready for the river," I reply. He swears saying,

"I'm f..... stupid." Then he's at the top of the stairs, "You can't go alone!"

The drive is endless, in silence. In the carpark, we dress in waterproofs, rods and bags and wellies on. He's grumbling… It is still dark, but I know it so well. I lead the way, he is chuntering behind me, I blank him out, a few birds are beginning to wake. I long to leave him but I focus on my footing, there is no phone signal down here and how would I tell them my location anyway? The river rages even louder in the half light. l pass the calm Reese pool and keep going to where I'm in a deep valley, the bank drops down, huge tree roots and over-hanging branches, I grab one and lower myself down onto the rocks. The river is at her narrowest here but two enormous oaks, one on either side of the river, reach out to each other, but there is a gap of several metres between branch tips. Their huge roots holding them fast in the exposed bank, like gripping hands. The light is just coming up over the hill, there is a loud rustle and a scurrying movement around the trunk of the oak, my side of the river. It's a grey squirrel, he watches me, dashes up the trunk, tail flicking and onto the longest reaching branch. "You can't be serious," I say out loud. The river rages beneath, white foam froths in the torrent of water. "You'll never make it!" I watch in horror.

In slow motion, but instantaneously, squirrel runs and leaps towards the outstretched branch on the opposite bank. I can hardly believe it will hold his weight. He spins upside down on landing, rights himself with his tail, pauses momentarily and with a cocky flick of his tail, dashes along the branch, and down the trunk, disappearing into the undergrowth on the opposite bank.

A leap of faith!

I feel the next stage of my life will be similar. I will make it as well.

I don't fish for long, a couple of casts with weight and worms. It's been a long and tiring night, and I can't put up with his mood much longer. I don't feel sad, back at the car, as we leave the river. I feel inspired by the squirrel!

I leave Wales and shortly after, his life behind.

"The Prince of The Palace"

I smile to myself as I drive through the archway of this great estate. Even more pleasing is the knowledge I have a year pass, all I have to do is show my card to the gate keepers, they smile and wave me through. The palace stands in all her grandeur at the end of the long straight drive, enormous gold balls decorate the roof, glistening in the morning sun.

The car park is quiet, it is still early. It is going to be warm, there is a cloudless sky.

The lake sparkles below the palace lawn, which slopes steeply towards the bridge and curves to the left out of sight.

I park my car, rucksack on my back, I head off for a walk around the grounds. At present, I live alone and work alone. This morning, I woke tired of solitude, I felt restless, lonely. I phoned my son, asked if I could pop over for coffee. "Sorry Mum, we're having a duvet day." I did understand, they are still new, wrapped in each other, literally.

Walking by the lake my spirit lifted. The path is tarmac, easy walking, I can admire the scenery and not my footfall, although there is plenty of sheep and goose mess to be avoided. Sheep graze the estate grasslands. Flocks of geese, swan couples and a variety of duck all gather in pockets at the water's edge. On the small island, egrets nest in the treetops.

The grounds were the inspiration of Capability Brown, I ponder for a moment at the water's edge as it laps gently on the shingle shore. I would love to have met him, walked with him, while he explained his plans in creating this landscape on such a colossal scale.

I walk with my hands behind my back, as I imagine he would have done all those years ago, creating.

Joggers pass me, dog walkers and running pram mothers, life in the fast lane from birth, I wonder, will the child staring into its mother's hot red sweaty face go on to be an athlete? I am in not such a rush, never was.

I walk for several hours. It is hot now. I'm tiring. I head in the direction of my car. I stop on top of the slope and survey the view. I have the perfect picture of the palace, the whole lake, the bridge and the monument, far in the distance, on the crest of the hill. Lunch time, my stomach grumbles.

I drop down the bank sideways, it's steep, only a few metres.

I sit down, the ground is welcomingly warm beneath me. The grass is short and compact from nibbling teeth, not a nettle or thistle in sight. I kick off my shoes, connect with the earth, my toes unfurl like fern fronds reaching for daylight. I look over my shoulder, the car park is rammed.

All around me picnic families spread out blankets, play ball games, children paddle at the water's edge, shrieks of excitement and dogs barking.

A group of teenagers gather to my left under the shade of the coppiced trees. Happy, relaxed laughter and music float up towards me.

Loneliness taps me on the shoulder. A damp rented annex awaits me. I sigh, it could always be worse. I raise my head up and let the sun warm my face, a gentle breeze strokes my hair.

I left a loveless relationship. I think how far I've come, and not just today.

I'm on my third move, no fourth! Gosh, I shock myself with this realisation. Every day is a winding road, I hum, a tune that fills the radio waves at present. First, I had a tiny room on work premises, then I stayed with a friend in another county. Then, on a

"The Prince of The Palace"

farm for recuperating racehorses, which ever window I looked out of, magnificent horses grazed. And now the annex. My life is mostly in storage, scattered, but I have what I need. I'm free, I'm healthy, my son is happy, I'm earning money, I can pay the rent and I have my paints. Mainly I paint on slate, Zebras, endless Zebras, because black and white is how I feel, there is no colour in me at present.

I watch as more families arrive, and I envy what I think they have.

I let out a deep sigh, and take out my sandwich and flask from my rucksack.

Everyone has the same idea, ball games and exploring end, families gather on their blankets, food and drink is passed around, quiet low chatter replaces the excitement of earlier.

I take a bite of my sandwich, ham and mustard, it's warm and a bit limp, but tasty, most welcome. I have a sudden overwhelming feeling I'm not alone, and as I take my second bite, I look over the top of my sandwich. I don't move, there standing in front of me, barely two feet from my bare toes, is the most elegant of gentlemen.

Immaculately dressed, he must be the prince of the palace. Smart white necktie, rather red in the face, glossy green head, and neck with freckled russet plumage, and a long trailing tail.

Will you join me for lunch? I welcome him cheerfully. He tilts his head slightly sideways, eyeing my lunch.

"A crust for the upper crust!" I laugh and hand him a large corner. He grabs it, he hasn't got the best manners. I have never been this close to a live pheasant. He really is magnificent, every feather is breathtaking, I wonder what brought him out of hiding to join me, with all the goings on around us? I drink my coffee and share more of my sandwich with him. The last piece devoured, I roll the foil I'd packed it in, into a tight ball and drop it into my rucksack. I believe in always leaving a place with nothing but my footprint. My stepmother once told me, I was the best guest to have, because she would never know I had been. I am very proud of this fact. Picnic over, mirroring Cinderella at midnight, he turns tail, and at a sprint, dashes down the hill towards the woodland area, vanishing into the gloom without a trace.

Loneliness gone, I lay back with my head on my rucksack, and doze in the warm afternoon sun. I had lunch with a pheasant, I smile, I wasn't expecting that. Envy of the others here, fades into insignificance. I stay for hours on the grass bank, lying on my front watching everything. I read but I'm not really absorbing anything. I heal slowly in the peace and tranquillity. Families pack up and the car park empties.

That evening, I get out my paints, and on a long slate I paint a beautiful cock pheasant. There is colour in my work, I'm pleased. Months later, I gave him to a game keeper, who works on large estate, not far from the palace, in exchange for beautiful fallow deer antlers.

Magic happens all the time, as I put down my pen from writing this story, my doorbell rings. It is my beautiful neighbour, standing on the doorstep, with a homemade fresh from her oven, sourdough loaf.

Time for a ham sandwich. Perfect timing.

Enquiring Mind

Spring has well and truly sprung. It is early April. Everywhere is green again, full of new life, reaching towards the sun's dazzling rays. It is quiet and still the time of the cat, they are still hunting in the fields, and balanced on fence posts. Once the dog walkers appear, they vanish without a trace, for a comforting lap or windowsill. I am out with my two dogs, they are busy, noses down, reading and leaving messages in the grass, up posts, everywhere. Just bird song, trills and tweets, all trying to outdo each other, in their haste for a mate.

My path follows the Oddford Brook though a park and play area, here the brook disappears into a three-foot-wide tunnel, underneath the main path that runs along the Nadder River. As the brook leaves the tunnel, the Nadder giving her no choice, steers her left and she is taken with the flow.

There is often a brook trout at this spot, somehow, I imagine the turbulence caused with two waters meeting must massage him. Any vibration disturbs him, and he darts for the darkness of the opposite bank, where over hanging trees give shelter, always returning once the danger has passed by.

A low wall with white painted railings, steer the river towards the churchyard and the old Brewery. I drape myself over them, they are ice cold and drip with dew. The field beyond the opposite bank is overgrown and ungrazed, small trees margin the bank. A black poo bag hangs from one of the top branches. Why is man so destructive?

The water level is low, and the exposed bank reveals holes and burrows.

I wonder how the water voles have fared this winter? "I hope you are alright Mr Vole. I haven't seen you this year?" I enquire, with that, there's a plop! I'd know that plop anywhere, and there he is Mr Vole swimming directly towards me, about the size of a tennis ball, and nearly as round, tiny alert beady black eyes lock with mine, little fury ball of determination paddles across the river. He stops underneath where I'm leaning, this is where the brook meets the Nadder so he has to paddle hard in the turbulence. I can't stop smiling, we stare at each other, just a few seconds, then he turns back in the direction he came, to calmer water, and continues his quest to the opposite bank. "Did anyone see that?" I say out loud. I am alone and it would never have happened, had I not been.

So sweet, I'm so relieved to see him, it means the river is still healthy. The signal crayfish have found their way here, and are causing turmoil, excavating deep tunnels in the banks, and most of the greenery from the riverbank has long since gone. But Mr vole is coping.

My dogs come over to see who I've been talking to...

The Hazelnut Heist

A stone's throw away from my home is Nut Alley. It's a well-used footpath and shortcut. One side is sheltered by high, back garden fences, the other, a bank beyond which are larger gardens. Here there is a hazel hedge, and lush wild garlic grows in the spring. This year there is a bumper crop of the former. Their branches are laden with ripe nuts, like little fat men in tight jackets, collars turned up. Hundreds have fallen and rolled down the sloping path and crunch underfoot, all is going to waste. I sigh. I have decided to gather them up and make use of them. They are hard to crack open, with their thick protective shells, with a very tasty cream nut inside. So, with a rake and a broom, a sieve in hand, I spend the morning gathering. I wash them and leave them on trays to dry in the sun. Satisfied with my golden treasure, I line a large container with tea towels and fill her to the brim, I cover them with a large towel and push them snuggly under my coffee table in the conservatory. I stand back, hands on my hips, job well done... mmm, nut and raisin fudge and hazelnut cookies. The months pass by, and the nuts are all but forgotten.

It is dull and rainy, looks in for the day, perfect for fudge making. I check I have chocolate and raisins, and any ingredients I need. I walk into the conservatory, there in the middle of the floor, sitting alone, is one solitary hazelnut. Strange!! How did that get there, my dogs would never bother with them, even if they could get their heads in the container. I pull the crate free, it's very light: "Dear God! What the f...?". I pull back the towel, only a handful of hazelnuts, nestle in the corner. Frantically I search for an explanation, I look high and low, no means of entry or exit, inside and out. "How in the world and who? Where are my nuts?". Vanished!

Autumn came and went, the nights darken, and days are short. My fire burns and winter sets in. Then it began, I was reading by the fire, someone's playing marbles in the attic, it made me jump, I made the dogs jump, the hairs on my neck stood on end. It was as though someone was walking around in my roof space, in hob-nailed boots. Whichever room I am in, they seem to be above me.

Late in the night, they wake me as hazel nuts jostle and roll along the beams, banging and scurrying, backwards and forwards, only ceasing in the early hours.

Night after night, I climb into bed and lie there waiting for the shenanigans to begin, my mind and crazy imagination run riot, I imagine hundreds of mice and rats up there, or a few that have gorged themselves till they are huge, the unknown keeps me from lifting the loft door, the thought of being met, by piercing eyes and sharp yellow teeth defiant at being disturbed, keeps me below. Finally, I can't take it any longer. My son saves the day. He is going to WAR! Laden with traps and poisons he heads up the ladder, I can feel he is anxious, but he hides it well. I hear him moving about in the loft, in the corners and under the insulation. Satisfied, he comes down. "That should do it," he looks confident.

Within a few days all is quiet, peace resumes. How the little beasties got up there, still remains a mystery.

I will leave the nuts for nature in future, or only take what I need. I shouldn't have been so greedy. At least they left me a handful.

"Neil and Buzz"

Ring Ring, Ring Ring.
"Hello."
"Are you busy?" I hear a familiar voice, "Only there is a swarm of bees near the Donheads, can you help? The thing is! The bees will be in the car with us!" Knowing my friend and how long she has kept bees, I don't ponder long "Sounds like an exciting new experience," I reply. "Great! I'll be with you shortly, pick you up." I hang up, and rush to my sock drawer, and search for my longest thickest socks, an old pair from fishing days. I have a feeling ankle or wrist stings would be rather painful. As a child a bumble bee got caught in my mop of hair. I was stung on the top of my head, I'm not sure which one of us was more terrified.

Fortunately, I've been gardening all day, so I smell of the earth. Bees are not fond of the sweet smells of perfume or alcohol breath.

I watch her car pull up, she climbs out and goes around to the boot, to produce a bee suit. It's a good one. I slip it over my jeans, and tuck it tightly into my socks, and put my wellies back on. Gosh!! I feel I could walk into a SARS unit in this outfit. I must mention, all this gear is a mere precaution for me, being a novice bee helper. Many beekeepers tend their hives with little protection, and rarely get stung. A bee does not want to harm you, just protect the colony. In the case of swarming, they would have gorged themselves on honey, ready for setting out into the great unknown.

We only have to travel a few miles, along winding narrow lanes, the hedgerows are bursting with growth in greens of every hue. It is warm, early evening, breathless and still, waiting, needing to change.

As we drive, I'm given an update on the swarm so far. She got a phone call, late morning, to tell her there was a swarm in the garden. So, after bee suiting up, she had driven to investigate the logistics of gathering the bees.

As luck would have it, the swarm had congregated on a low hanging branch, calmly and quietly she placed the skep, a basket about the size of a wastepaper basket, only rounder in shape, underneath the ball of liquid gold producers, firmly tapped the branch, and they had dropped in. The queen, surrounded and protected by her royal subjects, were safely caught. The skep was then carefully turned upside down, leaving a small entrance space at the base, for those who eluded capture, they'd had the afternoon to locate and rejoin the swarm. We pulled into the driveway, the skep was under a tree by the garage door, smaller than I had imagined, a few bees buzzed around the base entrance.

A pair of heavy-duty beekeeper gloves land in my lap, CRICKEY! These will do in a chemical warfare factory. I slide my hands in, they come up to my elbows, but with full movement in my fingers. Hoods, with visors down, and secured with Velcro to the neck panel, we are ready. I can already feel my hair was not tied back tight enough, and a piece flops down across my eyes, irritating, I'm now behind mesh, and can't do anything about it. Gosh, it's warm inside the suit, humidity is high. We approach the skep, she drapes a large sheet covering it completely, and in one fluid movement, scoops it up into her arms. Surprisingly, there is only one incredibly territorial bee, prepared to sacrifice herself for the queen, she kamikazes herself at me, bashing on my mesh visor: buzz buzz buzz, she's angry. A few other stragglers fly around us. Quickly, the swarm is placed in the boot of the car, securely wedged for the journey home. As we drive, the hum from the swarm is unsettled, but not unnerving. I can't believe I'm in a car with a swarm of bees. Not how I imagined my day, as I swung my feet out of bed this morning.

As we drive through our village, and up the main street, it's quiet. It's the in between time, between work finishing, and coming out for the evening. We look like Neil Armstrong and Buzz Aldrin in our gear. One of the local boozers is outside the pub, alone, sitting at one of the picnic tables, watching the world through glazed red eyes, he's had a good time, but looks like tomorrow not so. He watches us pass, mouth open, head turning to follow as if watching a moon landing. We laugh! But also appreciate our good fortune, how many people get to experience this. Out of the car, skep in hands, we choose the quickest easiest route to the awaiting hive. Around the side of the house, down the steps, past the lavender, through a gate into the soft fruit area, under a large ash tree, finally through a small wooden gate and into the orchard. This is a magical part of the garden. The grass is long, wildness, paths are mown short and narrow leading across to the hives. Three tucked safely and sheltered just in front of a magnificent hazel hedge, East facing. Several old established apple trees, cookers and eaters mixed. It is perfect, quiet, and secluded for the bees to come and go undisturbed.

She explains, as we approach the awaiting hive, that I must hold the skep just above the top, once she's removed the lid, I must give the skep a forceful jerk movement, to ensure all the bees land inside the hive. Now I'm nervous, I've only one chance at this. OK, I'm ready, after three. I grip the skep tightly, the lid is off, with my firmest jolt the swarm falls, thump, a living buzzing ball. The lid goes down. The skep is empty. Relief! We smile at each other, job well done!

Opposite the hives, is an old wrought iron bench with gothic arched back, white paint flaking, it's a perfect viewpoint. When the apple blossom is in full flower, and the daffodils trumpet the sun, it is bee paradise. A fallen tree trunk lies decaying, close to the hive nearest the gate, mosses and ferns grow on and around, and a small Christmas tree battles for space.

A fine mistle rain begins to fall, we are very warm in our suits. My forehead and nape of my neck are damp with perspiration. Slowly, the air cools and the earth smells good, respite from the days intense heat. A peaceful, content magical humming radiates from the hive, we stand close, silent, almost becoming part of it ourselves. A moment that will stay with me all my life.

A few scout bees are investigating the entrance to the hive.

The next few days are vital. The bees may decide this is not where they want to call home and will swarm again. But I don't believe this is their intention.

We gather up the equipment, and head up the garden, leaving them to settle into their new home.

Good news, they did stay and make the orchard home, and produced a wonderful 'honey haul'. Now when I'm in my garden, visited by bees, I wonder, have we already been acquainted?

It is April 21 2020, A plague is upon us.

It is almost eleven AM. Within the hour, I drive to the vet, to have my dog put to sleep. I inherited her five years ago, when my mother died. She is an old girl now, and her organs are failing. I know this because we had a blood test yesterday, results not good. Because of social isolating, I have to leave her in the car, stand away, and let the vet take her. We returned home with a dose of antibiotics, but realistically there is no improvement. We have a restless night.

I have made a cosy area in the conservatory for her to lie, she does settle, and is sleepy, I leave her be.

The world is in lockdown, enduring a pandemic, COVID-19, a virus that affects your lungs, brain, and organs. I have now lost track of the days of the lockdown, the only days of any importance is a Thursday, when at eight PM, we all open our front doors, and cheer and clap, and bang on pans, to thank all the people who are keeping England functioning, be it from the rubbish being collected, to the doctors and nurses on the front line, risking their lives for those infected. We have no idea of the outcome. The news is full of blame and complaint of how it is being dealt with, while the death toll rises. From lunchtime today, it really will be isolation, when I leave my dog behind. We can only do our best.

Hard to believe, not so long ago, my dearest friend came to stay with her Jack Russell, we took the dogs down to the Dorset coast, and took lovely photos of the two of them on the rocks, waves crashing behind.

In time, I will paint that scene, one for each of us. The Lily of the Valley are in flower, at least two weeks earlier than last year.

I watch her as she lies by the step, head never quite resting. Am I making the right decision?... her body trembles.

I go and put her bed in the car, and start the engine, it ticks over, 'relief', it didn't on Sunday, the battery was flat. A very pleasant AA man started it up. It was the first face-to-face conversation I had had in weeks, I had to leave it charging on the driveway for an hour.

I've come back in and find her in the bedroom doorway, there is a trail of pale blood where she is standing. There is no choice. So many thoughts in my head. Because of social isolating, I most probably won't be with her in her last moments. I can't swallow. I tell myself of the already thousands of families, who are losing loved ones, under the same blue sky, does it help?

It is now two PM. What a lot has happened in such a short time, and where my mind has gone.

Ten minutes before I left for the vet, a dear friend, Alan, phoned. He told me calmly, as he always does, that an unprepared for, unexpected end was not an option.

I drove through tears, wanting desperately, once it was over, to drive and be with Alan, just a pair of comforting arms... bugger this virus. I pulled into the vet car park, and waved my arrival through the window, as instructed, and sat in the back of the car with her, big black eyes looked up at me, I kissed her many times. A young vet, different from yesterday, came out and I had

to sign a consent form. I just wanted a simple box with her ashes, easy to scatter. He explained it would be possible but awkward for me to be present, it would have to be through IV because he couldn't have a nurse with him, I let him take her away in his arms, I couldn't look.

The thought of going home filled me with dread. I drove to the supermarket; first time since the virus hit. To my complete

It is April 21 2020. A plague is upon us.

amazement, there was no queue. I got a trolley and was instructed to follow the arrows around the store. Keeping distances marked. But there were more staff visible than customers. I got champagne to celebrate her life, gin to drown mine, and scotch because I could. As I came down the pet aisle, I turned my attention away, realising I didn't have to rush, no little dog waiting in the car.

At the checkout was a lovely optimistic chap, going to be eighteen in a day or so, I was his last customer for the day shift. "It will be over soon," I can hear him now. I smiled. I drove home with the window down, the warm wind whirling around my neck and shoulders, it felt so good. I feel relief her pain is over, but as I enter my home, with no one to greet me, or nose in my shopping bag, almost tripping me up, I feel my loss. It's going to be very different. I'm going for a walk alone!

It was a good walk. But my legs were tired as soon as I set off, it's been a journey today. I met my neighbour at the station, she was very sad at my news. I met another chap I know. "NO DOG?", I know I will have to hear this many more times.

I haven't moved the dog bed or water bowl. I noticed the unwelcome poos on the flagstones, by the gate. I think of her back with my mother, she's sitting back on her legs as she always had, barking, and bossing her about. My mother is stroking her. "Well, she could have groomed you first," I smile.

As for my head right now! I want to be with Alan, soaking in a huge bubble bath. I will rest in between his legs and lie back on his chest, prrr.

Sunday now, time passes. I sometimes think I see her, or hear her paws on the kitchen floor. I even woke, thinking she was on the end of the bed. I haven't cried again; grief is like sneezing, unexpected.

The collard doves have come down for a bath; it's empty. I fill it from the water butt. First to show is Mr Sparrow, he does under his armpits. The pigeons are cooing romantically, I think they are going to have a shag before their bath, sensible! Chance would be a fine thing. All we hear is coronavirus and death rates, my girlfriend said, "She missed us dancing and having a drink!" I'll have a T-shirt made saying 'Oh! For a STD'.

We laugh till we ache.

Flypast

Click, Click, Click, Click, Click.

Shit! What have I done? I'm down by my pond, cutting back the sedge, growing at the water's edge, before she spreads her seed.

I thought all the dragonflies had emerged, transformed, and taken flight. There is an unmistakable sound of large wings tapping against the undergrowth, it can only be a dragonfly. The sound reminds me of my childhood, packet gliders made from balsa wood, set free by winding an elastic band around the propeller.

I spot her, she is just above the water surface, but her abdomen is curled under her, and one of her wings is bent at the tip. "I thought you had all gone," I tell her or him, probably a him, males in nature are far more beautiful.

I take my sandal off, only thing to hand, as urgence is required, she can't get any wetter. I managed to get my shoe under her, and her on to it, she's shocked but stays remarkably still. I cover her with my other hand, and rush to the conservatory. I pick her up, a very strange feeling, and lay her gently on the arm of the chair, in full sun, to heal and dry. What a shame, I hadn't spotted her before I started chopping. She's probably been in my pond possibly three years, under water, as one of the most dangerous predators there. Now, her weather forecast good, she has hauled herself out during the night, in nymph form, crawled up a stem; in first light, pulled herself out of a dark brown ugly dying corpse, to emerge as a beautiful iridescent dragonfly.

I have watched many drying in the sun, wings unfurling, gently vibrating, like a tiny aeroplane engine waiting for take-off. A very

When Nature Nurtures

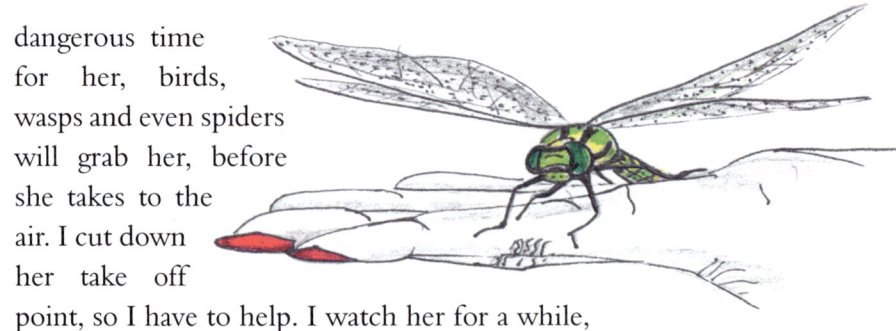

dangerous time for her, birds, wasps and even spiders will grab her, before she takes to the air. I cut down her take off point, so I have to help. I watch her for a while, but I'm cooking a pavlova for the village lunch, I check her periodically.

Click, click, click, click, click, her wings clatter.

I rush to the door, NO SIGN OF HER! I swear again, only much worst. She has dropped down on the floor, behind planted pots, has cobweb on her, and is more bent than before... more cursing!

I lift her by her torso, and place her on a thick back of a chair, only a few feet from the open doorway, in full sun, I point to the door, and give hand signals like a flight attendant 'fly this way', I instruct. She, at this moment, doesn't look like she is going anywhere fast. Huge bulbous eyes watch me. "I'm worried a bird might come in and take you," is she listening? The other alternative is plants and more cobwebs, and wing-damaging peril.

I keep popping out to check on her, between whipping cream and preparing myself.

It's a miracle! In just over an hour, her abdomen has straightened, and her wings are outstretched and perfectly formed. We stare at each other, me in wonder, how does she see me? I hope she's not afraid. I tell her, "I haven't got long, I have to go out. I leave her and put on my mascara." Oh!! You've gone, vanity made me miss her take off. I feel exhilarated then slightly sad.

Pavlova in my grasp, I head for the village hall. There is a shortcut that runs along the brook, I've seen eels in there, big eels, but that's another story. A few hundred yards along, the brook meets the mighty Nadder river, one of five rivers that unite in the meadows of Salisbury, Nadder of old English means 'snake'. As the path ends, there are large, tall laurels that edge the path, and block the view of the brook, and opposite, the garden fences are tall; this doesn't leave much room for manoeuvre, if you're walking your dog or meet someone coming the other way.

I stop in my tracks, suddenly in front of me, is a dragonfly, eye level she hovers momentarily, a moment in time we lock eyes. She turns and flies past me again, so close in this already confined space, I can feel her buzz as she zooms past. She turns at the end of the hedge and comes back for another 'flypast'. "It's you, thank you for showing me you!" I laugh out loud, still clutching my Pavlova. I hope nobody's watching, they might not have seen my dragonfly, just me laughing, and talking to myself, we don't need 'The crazy reputation'.

Her speed is fast now, I instinctively know it's final, off over the treetops, following the course of the river. I stand quietly for a moment.

That made my day! In my heart, I know it was her, she knew I would wonder. Nature is great when we're at one.

"Live well, my beauty," I whisper.

And the Pavlova was a great success!

About the Author

Lizzy Paylan was born in Putney and moved to Oxfordshire at the age of ten with her mother and brother. Fauna and flora have always been her means of recharging, and she takes inspiration from the constant discovery of nature. Throughout her life, she has sketched and written stories of magical moments and the wonder of nature. She is based in Wiltshire.